Origins

Blackout!

Jan Burchett and Sara Vogler ▪ **Jonatronix**

OXFORD
UNIVERSITY PRESS

Max

Cat

Tiger

Ant

Uncle Tim

Tiger's Uncle Tim made a huge model village in his back garden. When it was finished he invited everyone to a big party – with fireworks!

"It looks so real!" said Max.

"Have a look around," said Uncle Tim. "I'm going to set up the fireworks."

"There's only one way to explore a mini-village!" said Tiger.

They turned the dials on their watches ...

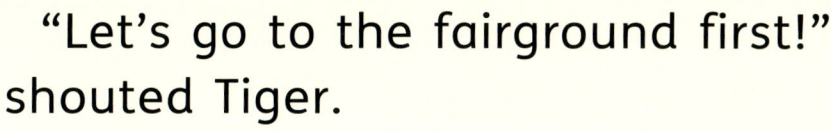

"Let's go to the fairground first!" shouted Tiger.

Suddenly, there was a loud BANG! The whole village went dark.

"Everything has stopped working," said Cat.

"Not everything!" yelled Tiger. He jumped out of the way of a model car.

"I think a light bulb must have exploded," said Ant.

"Let's find the broken bulb," said Cat. "Then we can tell Uncle Tim. Switch your torch on, Tiger."

Tiger pressed the button. The torch did not switch on.

"That's odd," said Tiger.

"Well, we'll just have to try to find our way without it," said Ant. "Come on."

"The bang came from over there, I think," said Ant. "Let's investigate."
The others followed Ant down the road, but they soon lost their way.

"There is a castle on a hill near the zoo, I think," said Ant.

"And the zoo is next to the train station," said Cat. "I think that's right ..."

Just then, a bus stopped nearby. "Look! It's going to the station," said Max. "Let's jump on!"

STATION

The bus reached the station and the friends got off.

"Where to now?" said Tiger. He looked around in the darkness.

"There's a sign here for the zoo," said Cat. "That might be a good place to start."

"Let's go!" said Tiger.

THE ZOO

They climbed over a wall, into the moonlit zoo. The models of the animals looked very real in the darkness.

"Come on," said Max. "Let's get out of here. There aren't any light bulbs in here and that lion looks hungry!"

"Let's try the castle next," said Cat. "I think it was near the zoo so it can't be far away."

"Yes, listen," said Ant. "I think I can hear the flags flapping in the breeze. It's this way – let's go!"

After a few minutes, the four friends came to a hill. Stone steps went up the side of it.

"These must lead to the castle," said Ant.

They climbed up, until they got to a wooden drawbridge.

Inside, toy knights in armour stood on guard along the walls.

"Wow! Look at these," said Ant. "They look so–"

CRUNCH! Ant felt broken glass under his shoe.

"The broken light bulb!" he cried.

Suddenly, a beam of torchlight swept over the castle. It was Uncle Tim!

"I must find out why the lights went out," Uncle Tim muttered.

"We need to make sure your uncle looks in here," Ant whispered to Tiger.

Cat quickly snatched two helmets from the knights and bashed them together.

"It's not loud enough," said Max.

"I have an idea," said Tiger, pushing a knight over. It crashed into the others. All the knights toppled over.

CRASH! CLATTER!

"What was that?" said Uncle Tim.

"Quick!" said Cat. "Pretend to be knights so he doesn't see us."

The children grabbed shields and put helmets on. They were just in time ... a huge eye peered through the window.

"It was just those models falling over," said Uncle Tim.

Max kicked the broken glass. It glinted in the torchlight.

"A broken light bulb!" said Uncle Tim. "That's what the problem is!"

Uncle Tim left to get a new bulb from the house.

"Quick! We need to get out of here," said Max.

"Let's use the shields as sledges," said Tiger.

They each grabbed a shield and zoomed down the hill.

Just then, the lights came back on!
"Quick! Jump in this car," said Max.
"No one will see us if we are in there."
BANG! BANG! BANG!
"Look! It's the fireworks!" said Cat.

When the car reached the end of
the village, the four friends jumped
out and hid. They turned the dials
on their watches ...

"Where were you?" asked Uncle Tim. "You missed the fireworks."

"No, we didn't," said Tiger. "We had a great view!"

For more adventures in the dark read *Cheeky Meeko*

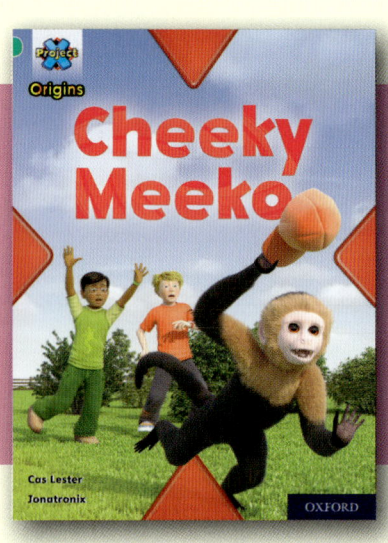

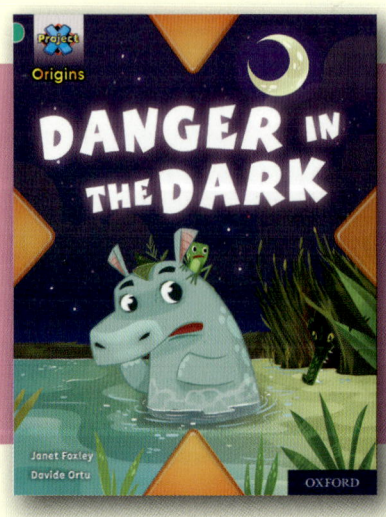

... and *Danger in the Dark.*